You Will Design Spaceships

A Combat-Fishing® Space Book
You Will ____ Space ™ Series
Written and Illustrated by
Bryce L. Meyer

Dedications: To any kid who wants to travel in space: let no one tell you what you can't explore in space. To future generations: put your boots on alien worlds!

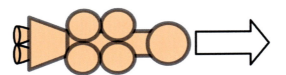

Library of Congress Control Number: **2015914644**

CreateSpace Independent Publishing Platform, North Charleston, SC
ISBN-13: **978-1516946358** ISBN-10: **1516946359**

© **Copyright 2015 by Bryce L. Meyer.** All rights reserved. No part of this publication, or its characters, may be reproduced, stored in a retrieval system, or transmitted, in any form by any means, electronic, mechanical, photocopying, recording, or otherwise without express prior written permission of the author. Contact the author in care of the publisher.
Note: there are scientific simplifications herein due to the audience.

The reader, parents, etc. hereby absolves the author from any harm or damage resulting from any experiment herein. IF YOU DO THEM, I AM NOT RESPONSIBLE.

What is a Spaceship?

Engineers are very creative people who use science to invent new things and to solve problems. If you are reading this, you can be an Engineer!

Space is the universe past Earth's atmosphere. A future home for people.

Design: To create a way, using science and art, to reach a goal. If there is enough math and science, designing is also engineering.

Spaceships are machines that take people or machines into, and around in, space. Engineers design spaceships.

Spaceships are like cars, airplanes, or ships, except spaceships move in space.

- Spaceships have a **space habitat** to keep the people (and maybe animals and plants) in the ship alive and happy.

- Spaceships have ways to move and steer how they move.

- Spaceships have a reason why they are built. A **mission** is a planned reason. A ship may have many missions. Missions include goals.

- Spaceships have lots of parts put together to allow the people in the ship do what the people need to do.

THIS BOOK IS ABOUT HOW TO DESIGN SPACESHIPS!

In this book we will learn the parts of a spaceship, and how the parts together, to do what we want to do, in space.

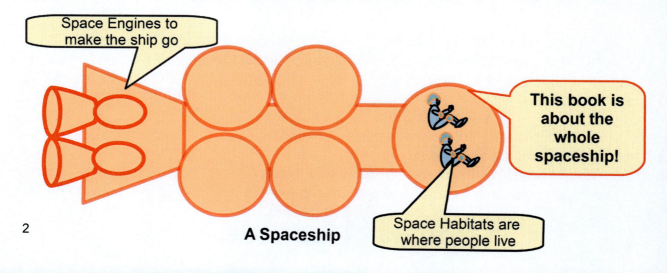

A Spaceship

Examples of Spaceships

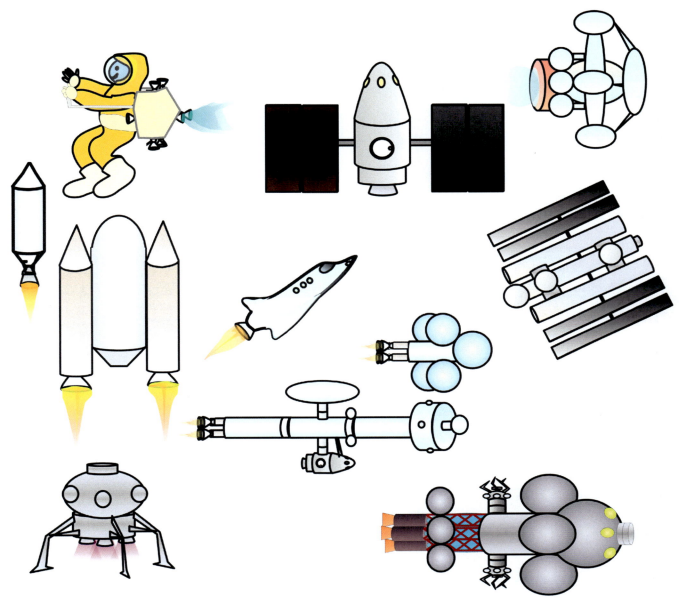

Spaceships can be put together to make bigger spaceships too. (An example from the 1960's is the Apollo Command Module, Service Module, and Lander.)

These are just examples, you should imagine your own kinds of spaceships.

Plan a Mission: Why Do You Want a Spaceship?

Missions are planned purposes for a spaceship.

What you need for this exercise? A piece of paper and pencil or a tablet.

Write down the answer to these questions:

1) What is the **name** of your spaceship? Make the name cool and fun. It is your spaceship after all. The name can be one word or many words.

2) If you had your spaceship **where would you go with it**? What is your spaceship's destination? Make up a name for your mission.

3) **How many people** would you bring with you? Are you growing food on the ship? Are you doing any experiments on the way to your destination?

4) When you get to the destination, **what will you do there**? How long will you be at the destination?

5) **Do you plan to bring anything back** from the destination? Will you go to another destination? Is the whole ship and all its stuff coming back, or are you leaving parts at the destination?

6) **What does the mission look like**? Draw a picture of a map for the mission. Use lines and arrows to show where your ship goes.

Example 1:
Hubble Space Telescope's Plan

1) *Hubble Space Telescope* ('*HST*' for short) is the spaceship, it will go into space on the space shuttle orbiter *Discovery,* which will drop the *HST* in orbit.

2) *HST* is going to Earth orbit and will stay there. The *HST Program* is the mission name, it is part of the Great Observatory Program at NASA.

3) *HST* has no people on-board. It is a robot.

4) *HST* will take very cool pictures of the Universe, and will be in orbit for many years.

5) The whole HST stays in orbit, and will not return to Earth as part of its mission. It will get fixed by later missions, but will stay in orbit as long as possible.

This mission is real, see:
http://www.nasa.gov/mission_pages/hubble/story/the_story_2.html

Hubble Space Telescope Mission

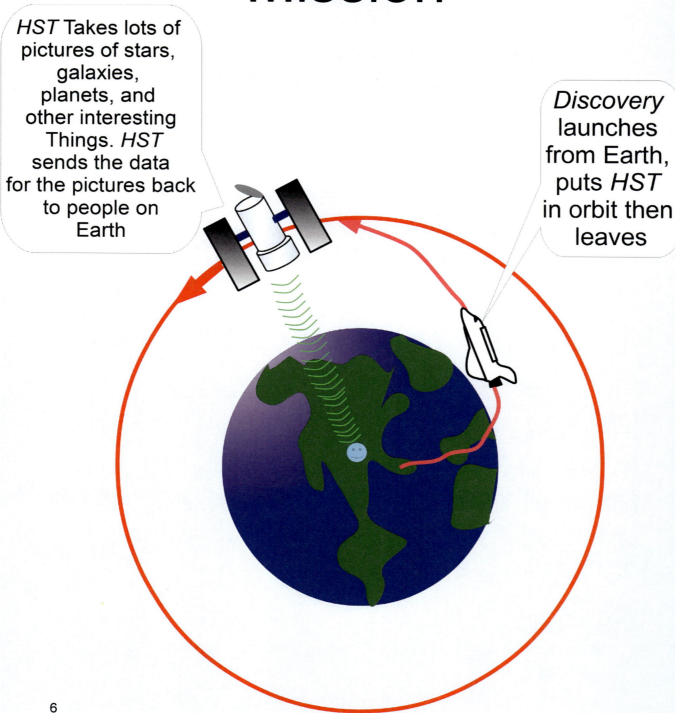

Example 2:
Asteroid Mining Mission

1) My spaceship is named the **<u>Piranha</u>**. *(Why? Because piranhas are cool fish, and nibble bites from bigger things.)*

2) The *Piranha* will leave from a space station orbiting the Moon to go to the asteroid belt between Mars orbit and Jupiter orbit. While in the belt, it will locate an asteroid with lots of gold, mine and refine 10,000 kg of pure gold, then return the gold to a space station orbiting the Moon. Once refueled and supplied, the *Piranha* will repeat the mining trip after 30 days at the space station. It might take 100 days to get to the asteroid I want to mine, 30 days at the asteroid, and 100 days to get back to the space station. The first mission is called *Bite 1*, the next *Bite 2*, and so on. The *Piranha* is intended to be used for many missions.

3) The *Piranha* will have a crew of 10 people. We will grow most of our food. We will recycle 99% of air, water, and human waste. On the way out and back, we will look for asteroids, and collect scientific data.

4) *Piranha* will stay at the asteroid 30 days to get the gold.

5) I will bring back 10,000 kg of pure gold, 400 kg excess food (just in case I need to travel longer than planned), 1,000 kg wastes, and 1,200 kg for all the people and their stuff. Total mass for the return is 12,600 kg.

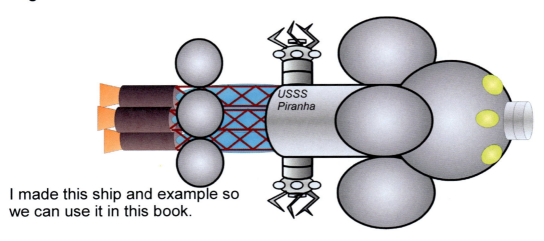

I made this ship and example so we can use it in this book.

Asteroid Mining Mission

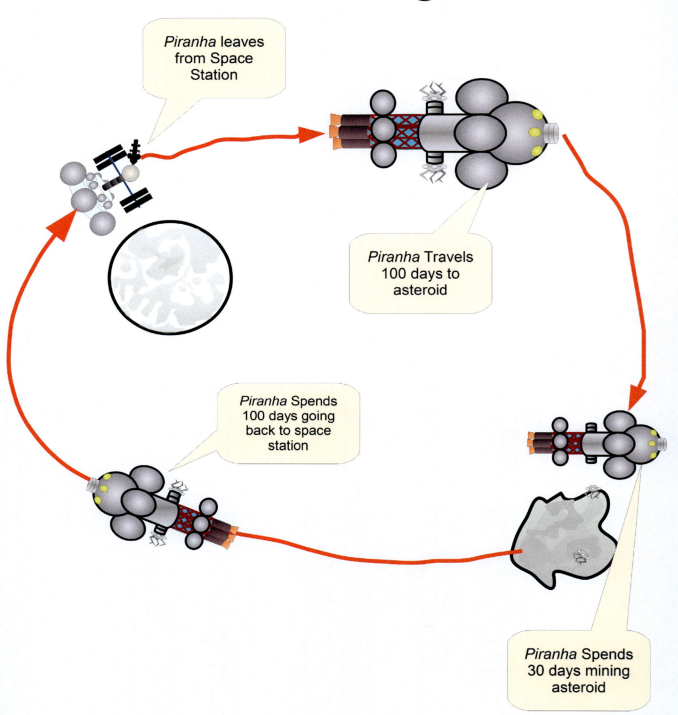

Important Words to Know

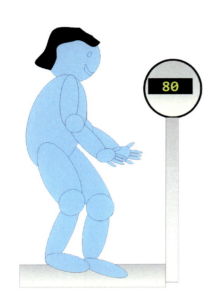

Mass is the part of everything that has weight when in gravity. You would weigh more on Earth then you would on the Moon, but your mass is the same in both places.

Volume is the space something fills up. A box has a volume of height times width times depth. A person takes up around 2 cubic meters if moving about. Gases (like air) change volume due to temperature.

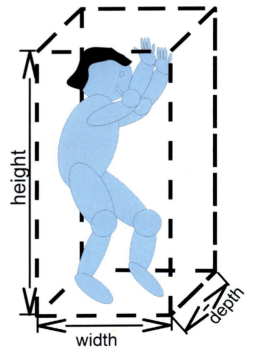

1 Cubic meter = 1 meter wide times 1 meter deep times 1 meter high.

You have both a mass, and a volume. So does everything else in a spaceship.

More Important Words

Speed (also called 'velocity') is how far something moves in a certain amount of time. The greater the velocity, the faster I get to where I want to go.

Acceleration is how much something's speed changes in a certain amount of time. The greater I accelerate, the quicker I get to the velocity I want (and the faster I get to where I want to go).

Force is how hard something pushes or pulls, and based upon the acceleration of mass.

Weight is a kind of force mass has when pulled by gravity.

Thrust is the force made by a space engine when it uses a certain mass of fuel or fuel and oxidizer.

- Spaceships use thrust to accelerate the ship to a speed.

- The more mass a spaceship has, the more thrust the engines need to make to accelerate the ship.

THRUST ⟶

Systems and Sensors

Sensors are things that measure and provide data.

- A digital camera is a sensor since it measures light to provide picture or video data.

- Other examples include thermometers, RADAR, gyroscopes, pressure gauges, smoke alarms, flow sensors, etc.

Controls are things that use sensors and instructions to make changes. Usually controls have computers.

- A thermostat is a control that uses a thermometer to change the air to a set temperature. People set the temperature, and the thermostat uses the heater and air conditioner to make the air the temperature.

Systems are combinations of sensors, controls, and other things arranged together, so that they work together, for a purpose.

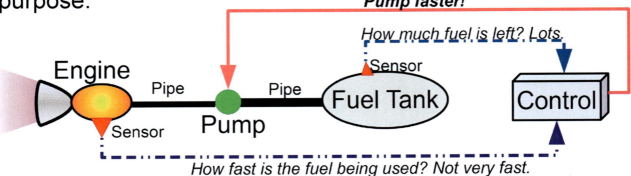

Note: A spaceship is a combination of many systems!
Example: The **Propulsion System** is a combination of tanks, pumps, pipes, sensors, controls, and engines.

Parts of a Spaceship 1

Propulsion System: The combination of engines, tanks to store fuels and oxidizers (together called propellants), pipes, and pumps, sensors, and controls.

- Propulsion: This is the push to take me where I want to go.

Navigation System: The combination of machines and computers, with sensors and controls, that tell the people on the spaceship where they are, where they are going, and how they can get there. Sensors like gyroscopes, telescopes, antennas are important.

- Navigation: Here I am. Here is where I am going. Here is how to get there. Here is when I will get there.

Steering System: The combination of machines, and computers, with sensors and controls, that are used to tell the engines how to make the ship go the right direction and speed, at the right times.

- Steering: Keeps the ship on a path to get me where I want to go.

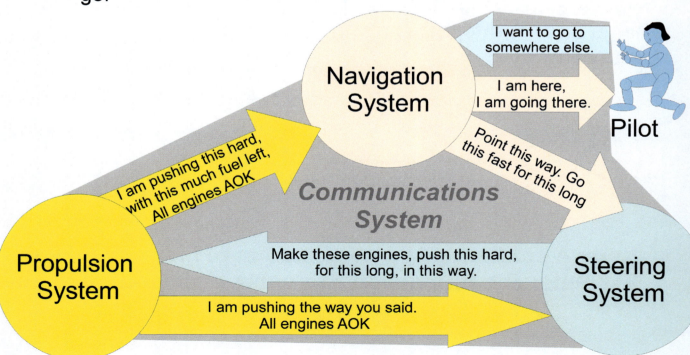

Parts of a Spaceship 2

Space Habitat (Life Support) System: The system that keeps the people alive, working, and happy. Includes space suits too. Escape included.

- Habitat: Keeps me alive and happy while I am in space!

Communications System: The combination of machines, sensors, and controls, to send messages between parts of the ship, between and to systems on the ship, or to other places not on the ship.

- Communications: Lets me and my computers talk to people and things in my spaceship, and to everyone else too.

Power System: The electricity or other kinds of energy to run all the machines and equipment on the spaceship

- Power: The energy to make the all the machines and computers work.

Other parts:

- **Mission Equipment**: all the things that you need to do the mission, that are not already part of the ship. A spaceship might have many missions at different times or at the same time.

- **Structure**: The stuff that holds all the parts of the ship together.

NOTE WELL: The same sensors may be used in multiple systems. **Reuse saves mass!**

Propulsion System

Propulsion System: The combination of: engines, tanks, pipes, pumps, sensors, and controls.

Engines are machines that make a spaceship move, by providing a force called **thrust**, usually using **fuel** stored in **tanks,** and usually moved to the engine by **pumps** through **pipes.**

Thrust is the force to move the mass of the spaceship and of all the things in the ship. The more mass a spaceship has or carries, the more thrust is needed to change how fast the ship is moving.

Some of what the ship carries is fuel. So if you have more fuel, you will need to use more thrust for longer times. As you use up the fuel, the ship has less mass, so can use less thrust or can go faster.

Usually the propulsion system is the biggest part of a spaceship.

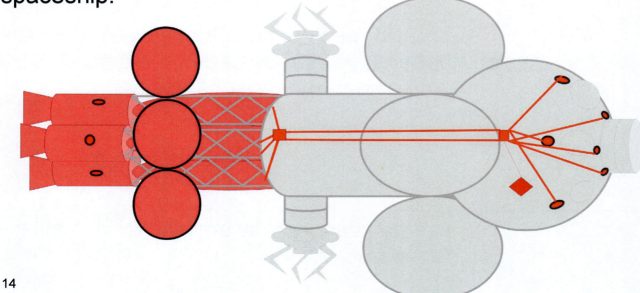

Parts of a Propulsion System

- **Engines:** The biggest engines are the Main Engines. There are also smaller engines for steering called **Thrusters**.

- **Fuel Tanks** (including Oxidizer Tanks, if any) to hold fuel for the engines. These tanks take up most of the mass and volume of a spaceship.

- **Pipes and Pumps** that move the fuel (and oxidizer if needed) into the engines

- **Sensors and Controls** to make sure the engines are working right, and so we can make the engines work the way we want.

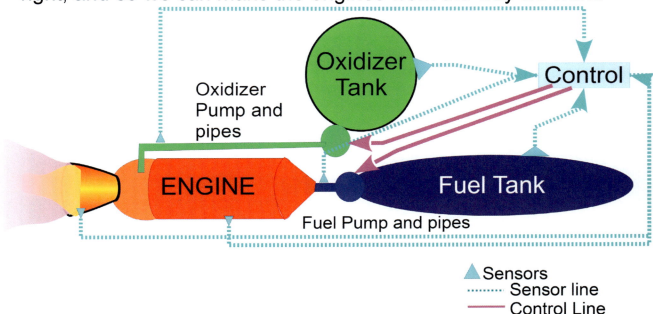

An inflated party balloon can be a propulsion system. The round part is the tank for the fuel (air), the nozzle and engine is the part where you put air in the balloon, and where all the air is going when you let the balloon go.

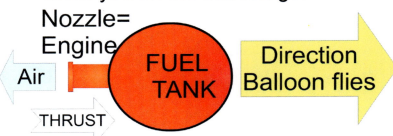

Kinds of Space Engines 1

Note: My book *__You Will Design Space Engines__* talks much more about engines for spaceships.

Cold Thrust Engines either use a fuel in a tank at a very high pressure, or use a pump, to shoot a fuel out of a nozzle. A party balloon is this kind of engine. Usually this kind of engine is used for steering and small movements on spaceships.

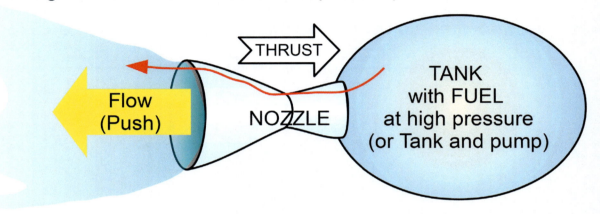

Nuclear Thermal Engines use nuclear reactions to make heat. The heat makes the fuel very hot. The hot fuel then expands and shoots out the nozzle with high thrust. These engines are used only in space, not on Earth. They can use many kinds of fuel, including water. You can get fuel for these engines from comets, the Moon, Mars, and other places.

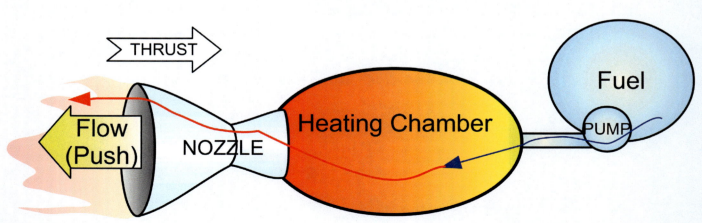

Kinds of Space Engines 2

Combustion Engines combine fuel and an oxidizer in a chemical explosion to heat and shoot exhaust out a nozzle. These engines have extremely high thrust, but use lots of fuel and oxidizer. The Saturn V, Atlas, Falcon, and Delta rockets all use this kind of engine.

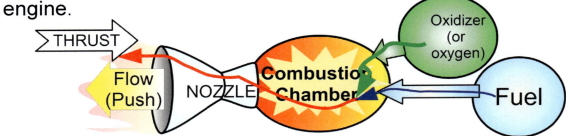

Electric Engines: use electrostatic forces or magnetic forces to make a fuel go fast out a nozzle. They have low thrust but make a spaceship go very fast over time.

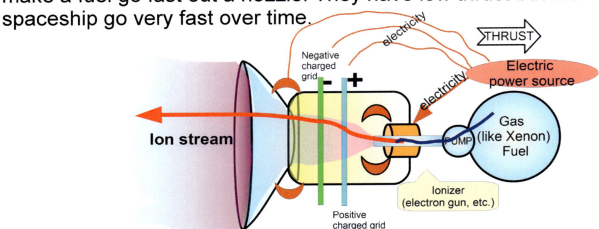

Hybrid engines are combinations of two kinds of engines to make one engine. The engines of my *Piranha* ship are one kind of hybrid engine (called Nuclear Cryogenic Engines) that combine a Nuclear Thermal Engine and a Combustion Engine.

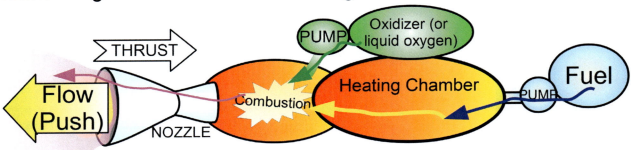

Spaceships can use more than one kind of engine.

How to Pick Main Engines

Here are things to think about for your spaceship:

- How far are you going?

- How quickly do you need to get there?

- How heavy will your ship be: when starting the mission, during the middle of the mission, and at the end of the mission?

Exercise: Think about what your mission is, and pick a main engine. Write your choice down, and why you picked it. This table might help:

Engine type	Where can I use it ?	Notes
Combustion	Main Engines and Thrusters, can be used anywhere including inside atmospheres.	Requires both oxidizer and fuel, lots of mass for thrust. Very high thrust.
Nuclear Thermal	Main engines, in space	Can use almost any fuel including water. Very fast with high thrust.
Hybrid Thermal	Main engines, in space	Can use many kinds of fuel, but needs oxidizers, very high thrust and very fast.
Electric	Main engines or thrusters, in space	Low fuel mass, but needs lots of electricity. Very fast but very low thrust.
Cold	Best for thrusters, can use anywhere with the right fuel	Uses lots of mass for thrust, cold exhaust. Moderate thrust.

Main Engine Experiment

We will make a rocket, and use a balloon as a cold thrust main engine.

You will need: a party balloon, 4 pieces of cardboard, tape, a short cardboard tube, and two paper cones, one big and one small (make from a sheet of paper and tape).

1) Make the two cones, take the smaller cone and tape it to the top of the cardboard tube.

2) Make 4 triangles for fins, and tape them to the tube so that you see a cross shape from above.

3) Tape the big cone to the bottom of the cardboard tube.

4) Inflate the party balloon (have an adult do this), but hold the end closed, do not tie it off. Release the balloon and look at how it flew.

5) Again, inflate the party balloon (have an adult do this), but hold the end closed, do not tie it off. Tape the big cone of your rocket to the balloon carefully opposite the nozzle.

6) Point the balloon rocket in a safe direction and let go of the balloon!

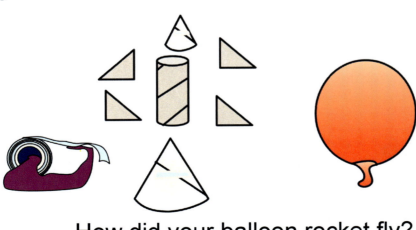

How did your balloon rocket fly?

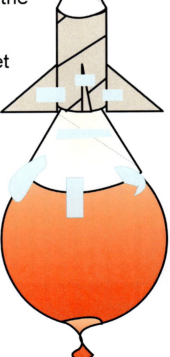

Thrusters

Thrusters are small engines, that may or may not use the same fuel as the Main Engines. They are located all over the ship, usually in groups. Each thruster pushes in one direction. In many ships, like the Space Shuttle Orbiter, they just look like holes.

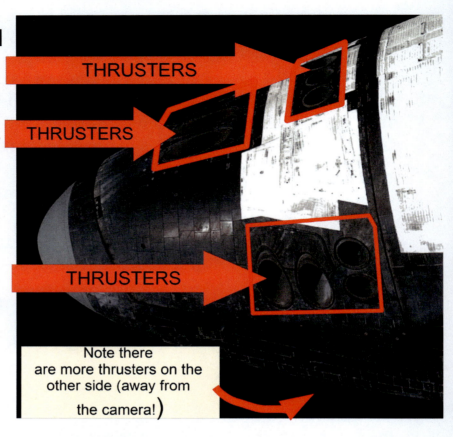

Note there are more thrusters on the other side (away from the camera!)

From: NASA S114-E-6215 (3 August 2005)

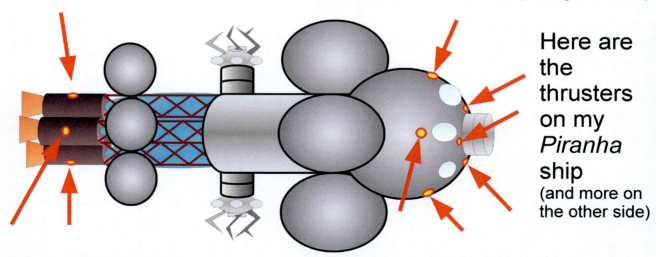

Here are the thrusters on my *Piranha* ship (and more on the other side)

In the Propulsion System, you will need to provide pipes, pumps, and tanks for the thrusters.

Where do I put Thrusters?

Where you put thrusters matter!
- If you could balance your spaceship like a teeter-totter, where would it balance?
- The balance point is called the **center of mass**.
- The "teeter-totter" flat part is the axis of thrust (where my main engine pushes)

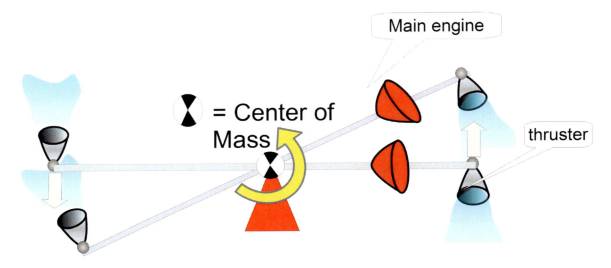

Place some thrusters as far from the center of mass as possible.

Usually a ship has at least 12 thrusters.

You need thrusters to:

- To go slowly up, down, right, left in both the front and back of the ship.

- To spin the ship around the middle

- To go slowly back, and slowly forward

Engine and Thruster Placement Experiment

This experiment shows what happens when you put thrusters in various spots.

You will need a straw, tape, sheets of paper or 6 paper cone cups, two chopsticks, chewed bubble gum or modeling clay, and 2 marbles. You will also need a very smooth flat and level table.

Steps:

1) Take one chopstick and tape it cross-wise to the other chopstick to make a 'T'.

2) Make 6 paper cones about finger-tip size. You can cut the cones off of a paper cone cup, or make the cones using sheets of paper and tape.

4) Use the bubble gum to stick a marble at the juncture of the top and bottom sticks in the T, then another marble at the end of the long part of the T.

5) Attach the cones as in the diagram on the next page. The model you built is our 'thrust model'.

6) Take a small piece of tape and mark a place about a meter in front of the long part of the model.

7) Blow through the straw into each of the cones, and attempt to steer the model to put one of the marbles on the marked spot.

Which cones turned the model fastest?

Which cones pushed the model straightest?

22

Engine and Thruster Placement Experiment
(continued)

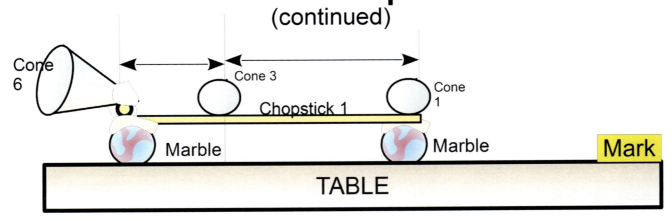

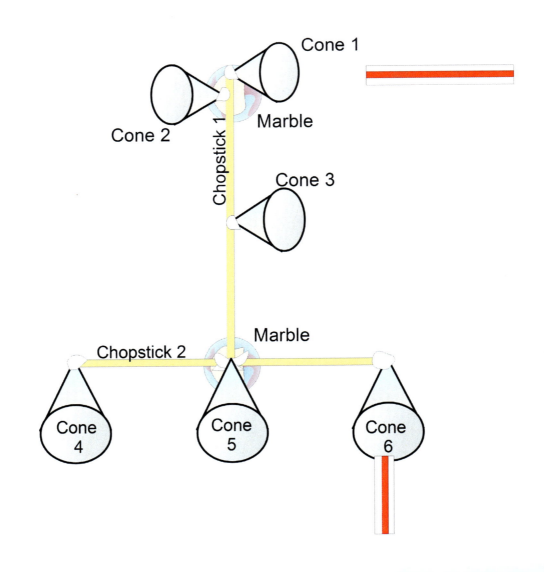

Navigation System

Purpose: To find out where I am, how I am pointed, where I am going, and when I will get there.

Since space is in three dimensions, and there is no gravity, we pick what we call up and down, right and left.

We can use **gyroscopes**, which are special tops, to choose what we call up and down, right and left. Gyroscopes always point one direction and stay pointed even if everything else moves.

Like sea ships, spaceships can use the position of stars and telescopes to figure out where the ship is, and where the ship is going.

If we are close to something, we can use radio waves or lasers to figure out where it is, and how fast we are moving relative to it and our ship. Lasers and radar are used lots for docking spaceships to space stations, and for landing.

The experiment on the next page will help!

Night Sky Navigation Experiment

You will need 2 friends, a piece of paper, and a pencil or pen.

1) Go outside at night where you can see the stars. Face any direction.

2) Find a pattern of at least 5 stars in the direction you are facing, and on a sheet of paper, draw the pattern.

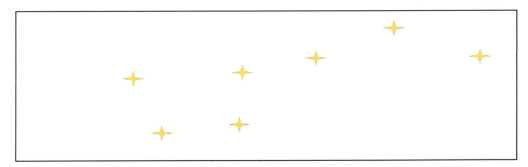

3) Have a friend (Friend A) blindfold you and spin you around a few times (carefully). Have another friend (Friend B) take a few steps away in any direction while you are blindfolded. Friend A should make sure you don't fall down!

4) After they remove the blindfold, use your star drawing to find your stars.

Night Sky Navigation Experiment (continued)

Questions:

1. After you took off the blindfold, what direction were you facing, relative to the stars?

2. What direction, relative to you and the stars, is Friend B?

3. Draw a diagram with you at the center as a triangle, draw an arrow pointing to your stars, and a circle (or a person) showing the positions of Friend A and Friend B.

4. Find another set of stars in your view. Can you describe the direction of these new stars, using the map?

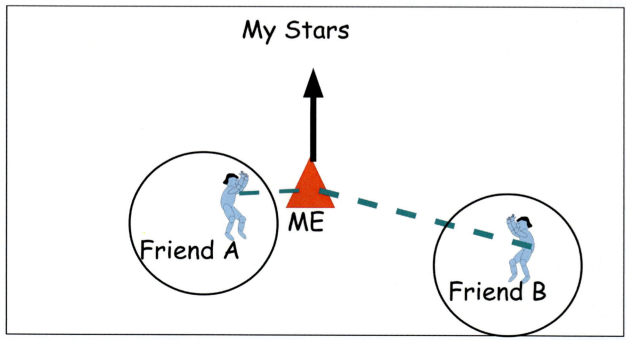

More on the Navigation System

All the information from navigation sensors (like telescopes, gyroscopes, and radar) is put together by computers in a Navigation System.

The Navigation System sends direction, speed, and location information in messages. The spaceship's Communications System sends the messages to the Steering System to keep the spaceship going where it is supposed to go.

Navigation information is also sent to people so they can pilot the ship.

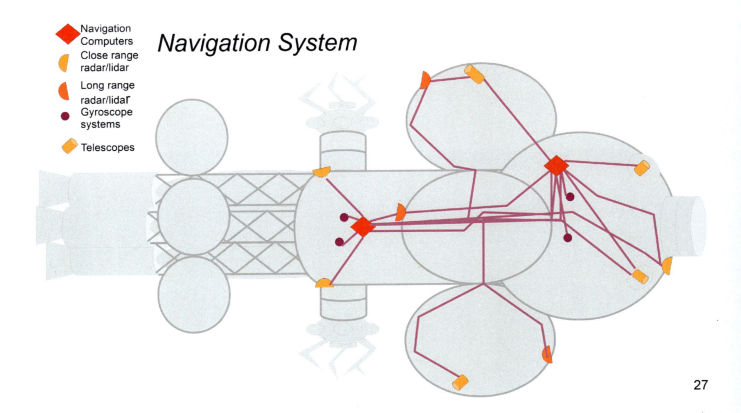

Steering System:
Getting on Course and Staying There.

The Steering System keeps the spaceship on course.

A **Course** is a plan in the mission that shows where the spaceship needs to go, and any changes to speed and direction to get to there. A **Navigator** puts the course into the steering system.

A spaceship **Pilot** is like the driver in a car. Sometimes the pilot is a person, sometimes it is a computer, often it is both. Pilots usually follow a course, but also tell the Steering System how to dock, avoid dangers, and land.

The **Steering System** will need to combine sensor data from the **Propulsion System** and **Navigation System**. All this data is sent using the **Communications System**.

The Steering System turns information from the spaceship pilot, the Navigation System, and the Propulsion System, into action messages. The action messages tell the main engines and the thrusters to increase thrust, reduce thrust, or shut down.

Combinations of thrust from thrusters and main engines make the spaceship follow the course and the pilot's commands.

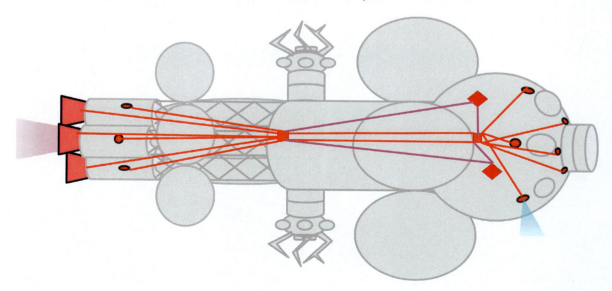

Space Habitat System

Note: There is a lot more information on Space Habitats in my book : **_You Will Design Space Habitats_**.

Purpose: To Keep the people on the spaceship alive and happy.

This system has:

- Places for people to sleep, clean, go potty, work, eat, exercise, and play.

- Ways for people to get to important parts of the spaceship so people can fix things, get to work, or get to other parts of the ship.

- Ways to keep the air clean and fresh, at the right pressure, with the right amount of oxygen and no poison gases.

- Ways to get and store water for people to drink and use, and recycle water from wastes.

- Ways to store, to make, or to grow, food.

- Ways to keep people warm enough and cool enough using heaters, air conditioners, and insulation.

- Ways to protect people from radiation and other space dangers.

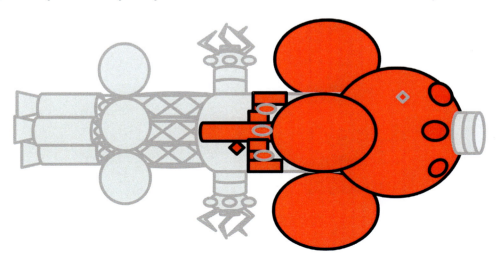

Habitat: What do People Need to Live in Space?

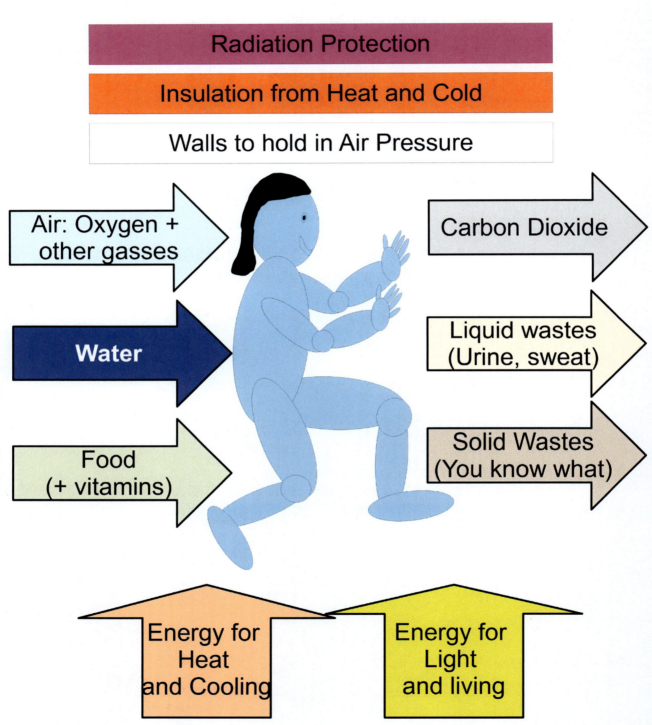

Spaceships are Moving Space Habitats

The longer a spaceship will be in space, the more room people need.

Short mission spaceships will recycle waste to food using machines, but spaceships on long missions might have farms too.

Spaceships that take short trips are like hotels. Spaceships that take long trips are like cities.

Spaceships may be the only home for some space explorers. People will live, work, play, eat, and be, together. They might have apartments on the spaceship just like people have apartments on Earth.

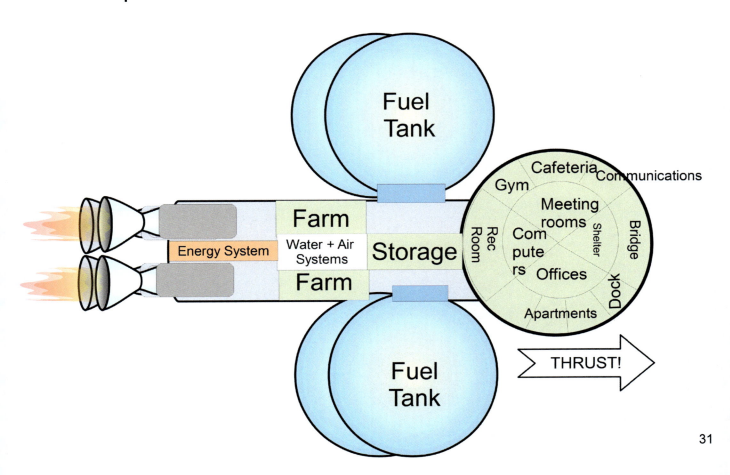

Communications System

Purpose: To send messages. The messages will be: to other people, to computers or machines, and between computers or machines. The people, machines, or computers, will be inside and outside the spaceship.

Communication to places inside the ship:

- The Communications System will have a **network** on the ship.

- A **network** connects people and machines. A network is a combination of wires, fiber optic cables, radios, and special computers (called switches and routers). The network connects all the systems, and parts of each system, together.

Communication to places outside the ship:

- To send messages outside the ship. You connect the network on your spaceship to somewhere else using radio waves or lasers.

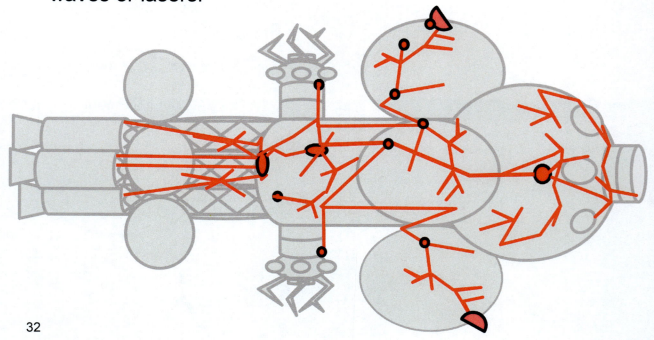

Power System

Purpose: To provide electricity or other kinds of power to all the spaceship's systems.

The Power System has these parts:

- a way to make power.

- wires or cables to send power

- switches and controls to send the right amount of power

- batteries to store power until it is needed

- sensors to figure out how much power is where.

You will need to figure out where to put all the parts of the Power System, including spares.

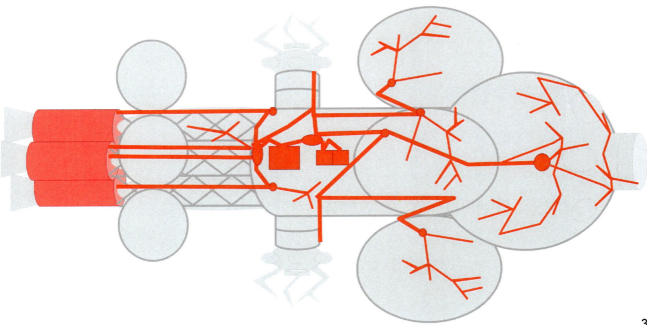

Power System: Generating Power

A **generator** is a way to make electricity or other power.

Some kinds of space engines can also be used to make electricity, but some kinds of engines use lots of electricity.

- Nuclear engines can make electricity when making thrust.

- Electric engines use electricity to make thrust.

Solar Panels can be used to generate electricity if light from a star like the sun is strong enough at the ship.

Nuclear generators such as fusion or fission or anti-mater can also be used to generate electricity and heat.

A very small kind of fission nuclear generator is an isotope generator. An isotope generator was used on the NASA *New Horizons* and *Voyager* space probes.

Fuel Cells burn chemical fuels such as hydrogen and oxygen, or waste gases from sewage, to make electricity and water.

If a generator can make heat, it can be used by the Habitat System to heat the air in the ship.

Mission Equipment

People need the spaceship to have many things to accomplish the particular goals of their missions.

Mission Equipment might include:

- laboratories

- smaller spaceships such as space suits, landers, pods, and robot probes

- robots for many tasks

- extra telescopes or sensors

Spaceships will have: volume to hold the equipment, electricity or power to run the equipment, extra fuel tanks or supplies to run the equipment, and extra thrust to move the mass of the mission equipment.

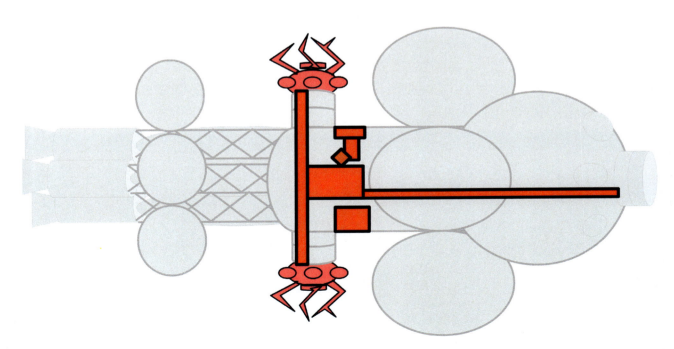

Water Balloon Experiment

Volume takes mass to contain. The water in the balloon in this experiment takes up volume, and has mass.

So, what happens if you have an engine (your hand) and try to move the volume and mass of the water in the balloon?

You will need a water balloon, filled with enough water to be flexible, not so much that it might pop. You also need 4 chopsticks or wooden dowels, and enough paper and tape to make a cone big enough to hold the filled water balloon.

1) Try to put the water balloon on a finger. Then push the finger up. What does the balloon do? Even if you can balance the balloon on your finger, what happens if you push your finger up suddenly?

2) Using paper and tape, make a cone big enough to hold the water balloon (or get a cone shaped paper cup). Place the water balloon in the cone and lift first slowly, then fast. Did the cone get crushed when you lifted fast?

3) Take 4 chopsticks or thin dowel rods, and place them along the edges of the cone, so that they meet at the bottom of the cone. Tape the sticks securely in place. Now lift fast where the sticks meet. Did the cone hold its shape when lifting the water balloon?

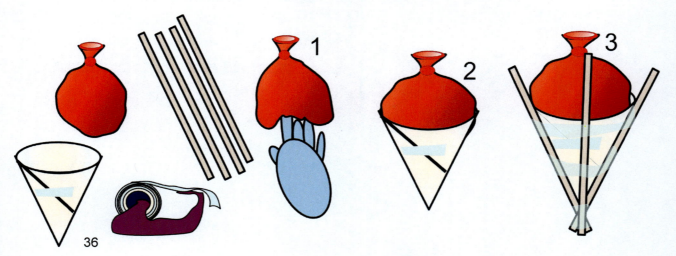

Structure: Walls

Structures are parts of the spaceship that keep other parts of the spaceship in place. Structures are the skeleton, membranes, and skin of the spaceship.

Walls: Walls divide the space inside a ship, and divide the inside of the ship from space. Walls are like the skin and membranes that protect your body, and divide and form your organs.

- Volumes are held in by walls. The more volume, the more mass the spaceship needs in walls. Spaceship walls are as thin as possible to be low in mass.

- **Outer Walls** are like your skin, the outside wall of the spaceship keeps everything in. Tanks have a skin, to keep the stuff in the tank.

- **Inner Walls** are like a second skin, to keep import things (like air for people) extra protected. Usually there are inner walls around the habitat. Inner walls can also be to divide volumes.

- There are inner walls around important and potentially dangerous parts of the ship, to keep accidents from damaging the habitat or other parts of the ship.

    - There are extra walls around: engines, reactors, batteries.

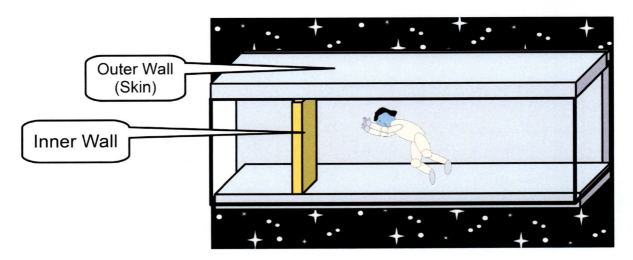

Structure: Walls (Continued)

Walls: Walls divide the space inside a ship, and divide the inside of the ship from space.

Between inner and outer walls may be insulation, shielding, machines, and places to run pipes, wires, and cables.

Inside a habitat people have walls to divide space for bedrooms, bathrooms, kitchens, work areas, hallways, and labs.

- It is a good idea to put some doors between rooms that can be sealed up to save air and people in case part of the habitat get punctured.

Walls can be solid, or have spaces like bubbles in foam, or have shapes like a bee's honeycomb.

- Honeycomb shapes are strong and light
- Foam and ceramics are good for keeping in or out heat and cold.

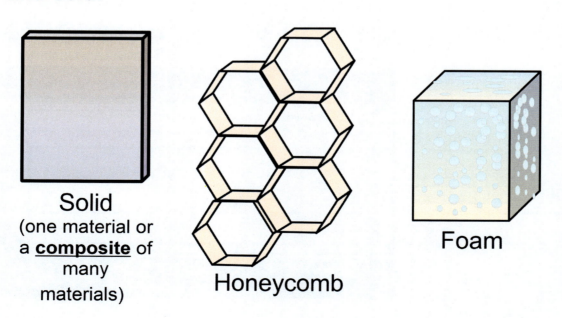

Solid
(one material or a **composite** of many materials)

Honeycomb

Foam

Structure: Beams

Beams are long parts of a ship that help keep parts of the ship in place

Like your bones. Beams are the bones of a spaceship.

Beams have different cross sections. A cross section is the shape that you see looking down a beam as if you cut it.

- A soda straw is a **tube**, which has a circle **O** cross section.

  - A beam can have a filled circle cross section, like a dowel rod or the food end of a chop stick. Solid beams like this are called sometimes called **struts**.

- I beams have a capital **I** shape.

- **Box beams** have a square cross section, as if you sliced a box.

  - A cross section with a filled square is a **bar** beam.

- Beams used next to the skin walls to strengthen the walls are called 'stringers'. Sometimes these beams have a 'T' shaped cross section, with the top of the T against the skin.

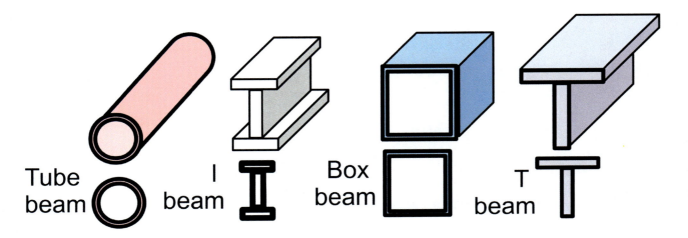

Structure: Trusses

Trusses are shapes made by connecting beams. Trusses are designs that combine beams so that the truss is stronger than the beams by themselves.

Trusses are like parts of a skeleton, an example in you is your rib cage. Another example is your wrist.

Welds join beams together. Welds don't bend but can break. Glues are used to weld beams, if the beam is not made of something that can be melted together. Sometimes glue and tape are used too (as in epoxy and carbon fiber).

Trusses can be made at the same time as the beams, pored into a mold to join the beams into a truss.

Pins (bolts) can link beams together, but the beams can swing.

Making 'X' shapes with beams, with beams on the sides of the X are one kind of truss used in the *Piranha*. Place these trusses on a side to make a strong three-dimensional truss.

Trusses can also be made by nesting spring shapes or round shapes together.

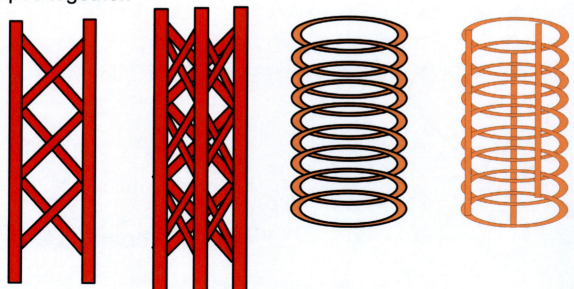

Structures: Overall

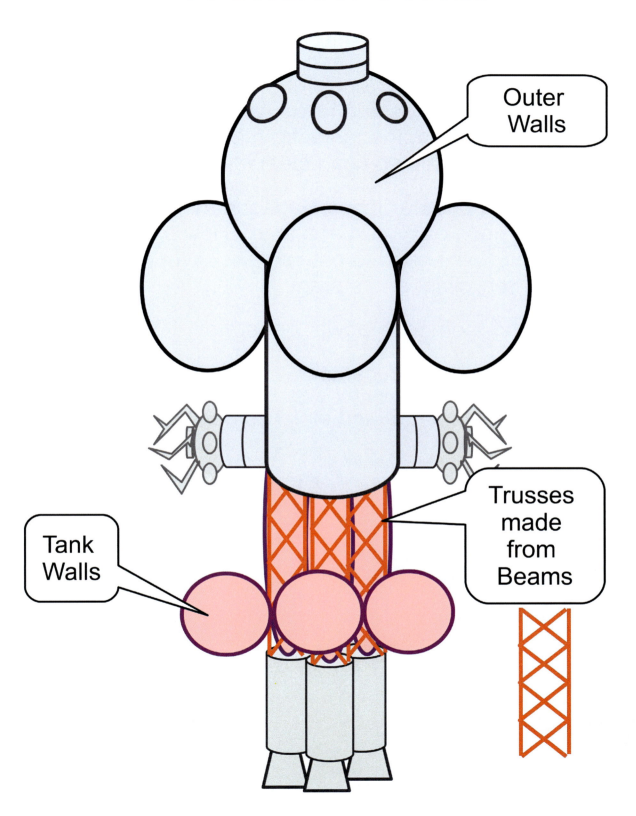

Laying Out a Spaceship

When building your spaceship think like this:

1) Where do I put the Propulsion System parts, especially the engines and tanks. Where are the main engines? Where are the tanks for fuel? Where will I put thrusters for my ship so I can steer?

2) Where do I put the Space Habitat parts. How many people will be in each part at a time? How much water, food, and air will I need to put in tanks? Where is space for farms, recycling, and storage.

3) Do I need room for a power generator?

4) Where is the control center?

5) Make sure thrusters and air locks don't get burned by the engines!

6) Where do I put trusses and beams to keep the ship together? Anything heavy should be in line in front of the engines, such as the gold the Piranha will bring back.

7) Wires, cables, and pipes are often put in the same spots, so that they are easy to access. Make sure you duplicate fiber optic cables, wires, and critical pipes. Put one set on one side of the ship, another set on the other side.

Laying out your own Model Spaceship 1

What you will need:

- A pencil and paper (to draw your spaceship).
- Any of these shapes: soda straws, cardboard tubes, Ping Pong balls, other hollow plastic balls, chop sticks or dowel rods, plastic water or soda bottles, string.
- Tape
- Marker

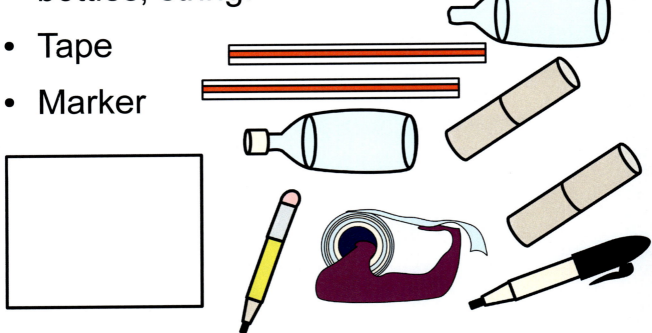

Laying out your own Model Spaceship 2

1) First draw a spaceship that can use the shapes you have available. You can use the mission you planned in the first experiment, or make a new one.

- Water bottles look a lot like engines and tanks.

- Hollow balls look like habitat parts or tanks.

- Tubes look like walls for habitats, engines, tanks, airlocks.

- Chopsticks, soda straws, and dowel rods all look like beams.

- Soda straws also look like pipes.

- String can be used for cables, conduits, and pipes.

2) Next, use your drawing to tape your ship together.

3) Use a marker to label tanks, habitats, etc.

4) Draw small circles on your model for thrusters

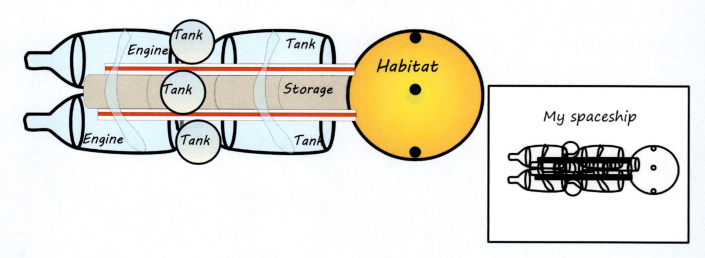

Questions to ask when Making your Spaceship

Where are each of the major systems?

- Propulsion System: main engines, tanks, thrusters

- Steering System: center of mass, computers

- Navigation System: computers, sensors

- Space Habitat System: air and water recycling and storage, food storage, sleeping areas, restrooms, exercise areas, airlocks, and hallways. Also, where is the control room so you can pilot your ship?

- Communications System: radios, antennas, on-ship network cables, computers

- Power System: generators, batteries, wires

- Mission Equipment: other ships, space suits, storage, robots, sensors, etc.

- Structure: walls, beams, trusses.

Put the ship together using all that tape.

Now that you have a model, imagine where it will go!

Cool Math: Volumes

The more volume my spaceship has, the more mass in structure it will take to hold it.

Volume (V) of a box is width (w) times height (h) times depth (d). If a box is 2 meters wide, 3 meters high, and 1 meter deep, its volume (V) is $V = w * h * d = 2m * 3m * 1m = 6$ meters*meters*meters $= 6\ m^3$. (m^3 is a short way of saying meters times meters times meters or cubic meters.)

A box has 6 sides, or in our terms, walls. Each wall has a mass. If the box is empty of everything including air, the mass of the box is the sum of the mass of the six walls.

Each wall has an area. Two walls have an area of width times depth, two walls have an area of width times height, and two walls have an area of height times depth. The area of all the walls of the box (A) is therefore $A = 2*w*d + 2*w*h + 2*h*d$. For our box above, the area of the walls is $A = 2*2m*1m + 2*3m*2m + 2*3m*1m = 4\ m^2 + 12m^2 + 6m^2 = 22\ m^2$. (Note: m^2 is a short way of saying meters times meters or square meters.)

To find the mass of the walls, let's say the walls have a constant mass for area, something like 1 kilogram mass per square meter. Math-wise, wall mass = 1 kilogram * area of sides of the box in m^2. In short form, wall mass per area (x) = $1 kg/m^2$. Then the mass of the walls (M) is in kilograms is $M = x*A = x*(2*w*d + 2*w*h + 2*h*d)$.

Problem 1: My spaceship is shaped like a box. It is 30 meters high, 5 meters wide, and 2 meters deep. For each square meter of wall, the mass is 1 kilogram (as above).
a) What is the volume inside my spaceship?
b) What is the total mass of my walls?

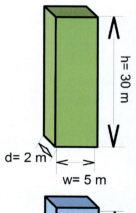

Problem 2: I decided to make my spaceship higher, its new height is 60 meters, the width is still 5 meters, and depth is still 2 meters.
a) What is the new volume inside my ship?
b) What is the new mass of all my walls?
c) What is the difference and ratio volume is my new ship versus the old ship? (i.e. New volume - Old volume and New volume / Old volume)
d) How much more mass of the walls is my new ship versus the old ship? (i.e. New mass - Old mass)
e) In words, as I have a bigger volume very roughly what happens to the mass of the walls?

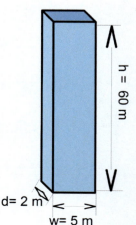

Cool Math: Answers

Trick: List what you have, then what you need, then equations that get to what you need. Draw pictures like the one I gave you earlier.

Problem 1: From the problem we know our spaceship is a box that is 30 meters high (h = 30 m), 5 meters wide (w = 5 m), and 2 meters deep (d = 2 m). We also know that wall mass per area, x, is $1 kg/m^2$.

a) We need volume, and we have an equation for a box, V = w * h * d = 5 m * 30 m * 2 m = **$300 m^3$**.

b) We know wall mass is mass per area, so we need area of the walls of the box, to get the total mass (M) of all the walls. We could use the equation for mass of the walls, given the 1 kg/m2 mass per area: M = x * A, where A= 2*w*d+2*w*h+2*h*d, so M = x *(2*w*d+2*w*h+2*h*d). It is a long equation, so let's solve the equation in parts. First, 2*w*d = 2 * 5m * 2m = $20 m^2$. Next, 2*w*h = 2 * 5m * 30 m = $300 m^2$. Next, 2*h*d = 2 * 30 m * 2 m = $120 m^2$. The area part, A, the part in the parenthesis, is then 2*w*d+2*w*h+2*h*d =$20 m^2$ + $300 m^2$ + $120 m^2$ = $440 m^2$. Now, M = x * A = $1 kg/m^2$ * (2*w*d+2*w*h+2*h*d) = $1 kg/m^2$ * $440 m^2$ = **440 kg** (the m^2 parts cancel out).

Problem 2: My new ship is twice as tall as my old ship, but otherwise the same: h=60 m, w = 5 m, d = 2 m.

a) Using the volume equation, V= w * h * d = 5 m * 60 m * 2 m = **$600 m^3$**. In short, doubling the height, doubled the volume of the spaceship.

b) Using the wall mass equations as in 3b, M = x * A = $1 kg/m^2$ * (2*w*d+2*w*h+2*h*d) = $1 kg/m^2$ * (2 * 5m * 2m +2 * 5m * *60 m* + 2 * *60 m* * 2 m) = $1 kg/m^2$ * ($20 m^2$ + *$600 m^2$* + *$240 m^2$*) = $1 kg/m^2$ * (*$860 m^2$*) = **860 kg**.

c) From Problem 1, part a, the old ship's volume was $300 m^3$. From Problem 2, part a, the new ship's volume is $600 m^3$. We are told difference is New volume - Old volume and ratio is New volume / Old volume. The difference in volume is $600 m^3$ – $300 m^3$ = **$300 m^3$**. The ratio of volumes is $600 m^3$ / $300 m^3$ = **2**.

d) From Problem 1, part b, the old ship's wall mass was 440 kg . From Problem 2, part b, the new ship's wall mass is 860 kg. The difference is 860 kg - 440 kg = **420 kg**.

e) Engineers are often asked to take a guess at a solution, without knowing all the data, using just their brains. In this case, you are guessing at the consequences of what you found out in problems 1 and 2. We call this a 'back of the envelope' or 'back of the napkin' guess. Luckily you already did problems 1 and 2. In part d, I didn't ask for the ratio of masses, but knowing that ratio helps your guess here: 860 kg / 440 kg which is almost 2. **A slick engineer would say: "very roughly, if you double the volume, you roughly double the mass of the walls, for a box shaped spaceship".**

Notes for Parents and Teachers and Anyone Else

Note, this book is easier to understand if you read the previous two books. That said, I made this book, the third in a series, for two reasons: first, I believe kids even at young ages, can learn some space engineering; two, space stuff is just plain fun and critical for the human species. I also want to inspire more engineers, and others who understand a little about what they see when they look at space stuff. Contrary to popular television, engineers are creative, artistic, cool, and smart. Some engineers are astronauts, and inventors, but also are: artists, rock stars, presidents, business leaders, physicians, lawyers, teachers, and many other very cool things. Most are moms and dads to good kids. Engineers are the real core of a growing economy. No building, car, rocket, computer, chair, or even soda bottle comes into the market without an engineer. Engineers start businesses that make new things. I also believe strongly that the future of the human species, especially if it is to be a happy future, requires that we increase the worlds where people live, and increase the places we can get resources, especially away from Earth where we don't have to impact nature to get things. Space, in short, is our future. I also enjoy making things, learning, inventing, and I try to make sure my nieces and nephews know that they can do anything, and that the path to anything may be via an engineering or science degree. Look for the rest of the **You Will ___ Space** $_{TM}$ series soon.

Other Books in the You Will ___ Space $_{TM}$ Series (so far):

- **You Will Design Space Engines**
  - This book tells kids how to rocket and spaceship engines work. It has experiments too.
- **You Will Design Space Habitats**
  - This book tells kids how to keep people alive and happy in space, including introductions to space farms, space stations, asteroid mines, and other cool things.
- **You Will Fly Spaceships (coming soon)**
  - This book talks about how to move in space, from docking with space stations to flying between planets and stars.

Other places to explore:
- My Space site: http://www.combat-fishing.com/animationspace/index.html
- The National Space Society Website: www.nss.org
- The American Institute of Astronautics and Aeronautics (AIAA): http://www.aiaa.org
  - Especially: https://info.aiaa.org/tac/SMG/SCTC/default.aspx
- The NASA website. http://www.nasa.gov
- **Your local library.**
- MANY, MANY, other places.

Made in the USA
Las Vegas, NV
10 December 2020